MOM2MOM

SUDESHNA KAR

To you, my mom, a beautiful soul.

With whom I shared all my joys and sorrows, my trials,

failures and achievements; and whose love, courage

and devotion has been the strength of my striving,

this book is affectionately dedicated.

Contents

Foreword *vii*

Preface *ix*

Acknowledgements *xi*

1. Good News 1
2. Postpartum 5
3. Get Back To Shape 9
4. Best Feeding 12
5. Post- Natal Stage 15
6. Healthy Eating Habit 16
7. Language Development In Early Years 22
8. Emotion And Socialization 28
9. Cognitive Development 32
10. Motherhood And Parenting 36
11. Quotes On Parenting 39

Believe In Positive Parenting 45

Foreword

I have known Sudeshna for the last 10 years, she has been an exceptional Educator and a caring mother.

She is a gifted special child trainer, who has provided help to children with special needs and guiding mothers to navigate through the challenges.

This book is a reflection of her commitment to further the cause of helping mothers through their journey. I highly recommend her book as it is useful insights and practical solutions.

I wish her all the best and look forward to many more.

- Mrs. Gitanjali Mukherjee

(Principal Glenburnie Group of Schools)

Preface

Life throws us a bundle of joy; it gets us off balance. As an expecting mother, I was away from India all alone trying to absorb the excitement and the responsibility that comes along. There were a lot of rights, few misses and a whole lot of sleepless nights. Wanted to share my journey as a mother, an educator and special child trainer. This book is not the final word of the best way but an attempt to give mothers a helping hand. The project starts with a faint line in a test kit with no end date. A mother will do whatever it takes, there is no right or wrong way, it's all about patience, focus and lifelong dedication.

Mommas you are not alone, let's share and empower ourselves. !!Cheers!!

Acknowledgements

Like all books, Mom2Mom wouldn't have been possible without the help of countless people who helped me along the way. There are too many to list them all. But a few have been particularly supportive:

My Parents(Majula Nag & Satyendra Nag): who gave me everything.

My Husband(Subhadeep Kar): my closest advisor and supported me every step of the way.

My Principal Ma'am(Geetanjali Mukharjee): who encourages, guides, and grounds me.

My Son (Reyansh Kar): who taught me the meaning of Motherhood.

CHAPTER ONE

Good News

The first magical news comes with a lot of excitement and impatience. Now a feeling comes that bubbles in your stomach, something you wanted dearly is suddenly there with you and the reaction is awestruck.

Is this really happening, it's not me anymore, something beyond me is going to happen. There is a life inside you and you are the creator. Becoming a parent is one of the most joyous moments in a couple's life. But, in the beginning, while testing the anxiety about the result really makes us feel as if we are a bundle of nerves. The two straight lines give you the happiness of shock, for a few minutes you take a pause and think is it real or in a dreamland? After confirmation, the news spread to the immediate family members and the discussion started. The world is a binary of 'yes' and 'no' 'dos and don'ts. Heart beats fast to jump, to dance to shout and the mind tells you oops be careful. It's best to trash all your anxiety, relax take a deep breath, and stay calm. Though it's a long and difficult journey the destination is beautiful.

Pretty moms may be suffering from morning sickness but it's lifetime happiness. Nine months of pain but a lifetime gain. Everyone wants a healthy and uncomplicated pregnancy. Medical supports are obvious but the most important vitamin from day 1 is "to be happy". The first trimester (0 to 13 weeks) is very crucial for a baby's development so consult with your gynecologist and midwife. After the first trimester, you step to the second then the third.

As a special educator, I have come across many children who have a varied spectrum of Autism. One common complaint the mothers reported as they were under a lot of stress during pregnancy. All of us are stressed, expecting mothers even more since they emotionally go through bigger challenges. Each person reacts to or manages stress differently. Ultimately a mother needs to find a way to move out of the stressful situation sooner before it starts impacting the baby.

If you are stressed, Momma does whatever it takes to feel good. Wanna have Ice cream, Pani Puri, your favorite soul food, a walk, taking to your best friend, whatever 'GO FOR IT. A mother can do anything for her child, for now, "Kick the Stress Out".

A few things to follow which I did will surely help you too for a healthy pregnancy:

- **Practice the mantra "Don't see evil", "Don't speak evil", and" Don't hear evil".**
- **Fuel your body with healthy and small meals.**
- **A healthy balanced diet is a must but occasionally satisfies your cravings.**
- **Chant "Om" and exercise daily.**
- **Take supplements.**
- **Be cool and quit smoking and drinking.**
- **Replace coffee with green tea.**
- **Take enough rest and pamper yourself.**
- **For morning sickness check which food suits you and eat little and often. Having plain biscuits and crackers may help.**
- **Avoid loud noises because babies in utero experience more of the outside world. They recognize voices, noises, and songs.**
- **Be aware of the warning signs like cramps and bleeding without delay** CONTACT YOUR DOCTOR.
- **Pursue your hobbies**

Prepare yourself for the blind date (labor pain where the date is not fixed. The best is pre-date information which will help to reduce the stress. The moment the child is born, you will fall in first sight love. You enter into the world of parenting.

"Pregnancy is not an Illness...
Going to Doctor
Doesn't mean you are Patient
It's the only happiness
That makes us impatient"

CHAPTER TWO

Postpartum

This blind date is quite contrasting where there are no candles, exclusive dishes, flowers, or romantic music but still, it's so special. Labor is the only blind date where you will meet your lifeline. Right after the birth, all eyes wait to get the first glimpse, and all ears desperately wait for the first cry. This moment is precious and indefinable. In this computer age, newborns are active, though their vision is blurry but look at the new faces, and react to the voices. The fingers and toes are like an exquisite flowers so fragile and so tiny but these smallest things take up the most room in hearts.

For the first time when the mommy meets her blind date is momentous. Those who are first-time mothers trust yourself, you can't be wrong. It's a lifetime experience and a wide range of feelings. Don't be guilty as your body has gone through a lot of hormonal changes. You may feel exhausted, tired, restless, depressed, and getting scary thoughts, please share with your family members, don't ignore them. Sometimes a feeling comes to the mother that after putting so much effort all the attention is for the baby but not for them. It's very important that during pregnancy the woman her husband her family members must be aware of the postpartum care because any woman regardless of her age, race, social, economic, the educational background can be impacted.

It may occur soon after delivery or up to a year later. The dads must support the mommies in this hard time. Share the duties, if the mommy is the night owl make her sleep in the morning. Give her sweet surprises, and take her for a dinner date. We all women love surprises and it's an awesome feeling when someone is making an effort to make someone smile. Postpartum means care, empathy, affection, balanced diet toward mommy which will pass on to the baby.

After I became a mother, my Gynecologist was concerned about my mental state. I had to go through the questionnaires during my postpartum visit like

Am I happy?

Do I get negative thoughts?

Do I feel hopeless or overstressed?

Am I trying to hurt myself?

It is a common practice performed all across the hospitals in the United States of America. The questions must be asked by the mother to herself because postpartum depression is a fact, not a myth.

My baby used to keep me awake all night. The zombie mom inside me felt often is this the life I have signed for?? Now, these are stories for me but have always shared my hard feelings with my gyno. Few things worked for my meatballs like a baby swing with water sound or a bedtime lullaby. Babies are often fussy which is natural. The soothing "SSSHHH" sound always made my baby calm. Find out what works for you.

CHAPTER THREE

Get Back To Shape

Breastfeeding means burning extra calories which stimulate the uterus to contract so it helps to get back to normal size. Breastfeeding means burning 500 calories per day, it'ssimply whoa.

If your Childbirth is natural and no complications, you can get back to normal daily life activities after two weeks. Will add to take the advice of your doctor as well.

For C-section childbirth, you need to be in touch with your health care provider and suitably take advice on when to resume normal activities.

It's best to start with a gentle walk and it's my belief that walking is the best exercise. After my delivery

it helped me a lot to stay physically and mentally healthy.

After two months I started light stretches, if feel any kind of pain then discontinue it for the time being.

Taking deep breaths helps the belly to expand and contract and the mind to relax.

One of the major problems I faced and many of my friends too was the loss of control over urination. It can happen embarrassingly at all odd moments sneezing, picking up the baby, U name it. Kegel exercise helped me to get control over my urinary bladder. It really works!!

Back pain comes in a package with delivery. Try Pelvic tilt exercise to reduce back pain.

Set a realistic goal like six months or a year because your body has gone through much, we must keep patience.

There are many more exercises. Be careful, give a gentle start. Our body compositions are not the same, you need to make a choice about what's best for you.

Don't comprise on diet during breastfeeding. A balanced and high protein diet is important. Eat whenever you feel hungry.

If your body is taking time to get back to shape even after sincere efforts don't be sad. We women are blessed, our body has done an incredible job, getting to shape is just another of them. Always appreciate and love yourself. Your

Baby is your biggest admirer, munchkin loves you In Shape, Out of Shape, No Shape. What Else.

CHAPTER FOUR

Best Feeding

Yes, breastfeeding means giving warmth to the baby, a sense of security, and rising the bond between you and your little one. Studies world over indicated Breastfed babies have fewer social and behavioral problems. For new mothers sometimes it's confusing if breastfeeding is sufficient for the baby if it's going to be painful etc. etc... The answer is simple, breastfeeding means you are giving the best food to your child which will boost the immune power.

After Twenty-three hours of the labor process, my Gynecologist advised me to feed the baby immediately because the first colostrum is highly nutritious and enough for the newborn baby. Was so worn out, I couldn't think of holding the baby.

As soon as my baby came to my arms, it was magical, nothing mattered, on earth, I got my heaven. Mamma this feeling is heavenly, the joy of bringing life. Sorry, let me get back. The Sooner the baby comes to the mother, the chances the baby will latch sooner and the colostrum gives the baby the best food.

Mother is:
M- Magnetic
O-Optimistic
T- Tolerant
H- Humble
E- Enthusiastic

Dos and Don'ts for Breastfeeding Moms

DO'S	DON'TS
• Make a feeding routine and follow the baby feeding chart.	• Do not overfeed the baby.
• Include right amount of protein foods like 2-3 times per day and have a balanced diet.	• Detox from alcohol and cigarettes.
• Exercise regularly (if you are fit for it).	• Avoid triggers of stress and anxiety.
• Take warm bath or apply warm compress to breast.	• Avoid unhealthy, too spicy and junk food.
• Wash hands and breast with a clean damp cloth after each feeding session.	• Do not take any pain killers or medicine without consultation.
• Always place the dark place areola along with nipple inside the baby's mouth while feeding.	• Without any consultation don't take any medicine to increase milk supply.
• Sterilize properly the breastfeeding accessories like breast pump, breast shield etc.	• Do not ignore sore nipples, any kind of pain from that area.
• Before going out express and freeze breastmilk.	• Never place only the nipple in baby's mouth, it will be very painful or may lead to bleeding.
• Use boppy pillows which helps to get the best positing for feeding both for mommy and baby.	• Do not keep or store breast feeding accessories in an unclean and hot place .
	• Do not keep your breastfeed swollen or engorged.
	• Do not force the baby to latch.

Take Care Mommies

CHAPTER FIVE

Post- Natal Stage

A child is born without language, skills, food habits, etc. Zero to six years their minds are like sponges soaking information in conscious and unconscious states from the environment. Every little thing that is happening around them they will absorb without any effort. Every word you say they listen; you act they copycat.

Careful parents! Someone is incessantly watching you.

Adopted Children absorb all their foster homes offer there is no difference between an adopted child to a biological child. For all my friends who went for adoption, today I can see no difference in their overall personalities.

It proves again environment is the best teacher, what you give is what they become.

CHAPTER SIX

Healthy eating habit

We know when we eat healthily, we remain healthy. All parents wish that their child has healthy and timely eating habits. Every parent makes their best effort to provide healthy food to their children. As a parent first we have to practice the same to make sure that our children make the right choice of food because when they eat healthily, they will live healthily. In short, what we preach we must practice.

I observed that children are not showing interest in food, if at all there is interest it's towards junk food. Subconsciously we are also promoting junk food for example for celebrations we go to fast food restaurants. It's a rarity, celebration by having healthy food. Finally, the kids associate good times with junk food, which is not their fault either. As parents, we know when we eat healthily, we remain healthy. All parents wish that their child has healthy and timely eating habits. Every parent makes their best effort to provide healthy food to their children. As a parent first we have to practice the same to make sure that our children make the right choice of food because when they eat healthily, they will live healthily. In short, what we preach we must practice.

I observed that children are not showing interest in food, if at all there is interest it's towards junk food. Subconsciously we are also promoting junk food for example for celebrations we go to fast food restaurants. It's a rarity, celebration by having healthy food. Finally, the kids associate good times with junk food, which is not their fault either. For parents, it's really challenging to inculcate healthy food habits in kids.

Enter Caption

Some easy ways to help children eat the right food:

- The best time to start solid food is when a child can sit in an upright position. The transition from liquid to solid must be slow and gentle and something which is easy to digest like rice cereal.
- Offer finger foods when your child is an independent sitter. Usually, the time period for babies to have finger foods is from 8 -12 months. Critical developments like eye-hand coordination, fine motor skills, and self-

feeding will evolve.

- Likes and dislikes start forming at a young age meaning when they are babies. Food preferences are developed early in life, so offer variety but never force them, just offer a few bites. One to six years are very crucial so this is the best time to lay the groundwork for a child's future eating.
- Encourage friends and families to offer them healthy food. Chips and chocolates can stay away.
- Encourage self-feeding. In the beginning, it's going to be messy but with patience, and practice they will learn to eat independently. Once they start learning to eat you will thank for saving your loads of time.

- Be the role model. Children imitate us so it's the best practice to eat together the same meal at the same table. Talk enthusiastically about food while eating.
- Allow them to touch to smell raw vegetables and fruits. Let them feel the different textures shapes and flavors. Make some sound like apple is crunchy and orange is

juicy. Engage the senses in their world of healthy food.

- Keep the serving small and feed according to their needs. Children must listen to their bodies and stop injecting food when they fill full.
- Take them to market sometimes and encourage them to pick some fruits, and veggies of their choice.
- Have some fun activities like matching fruits and veggies flashcards with real fruits and veggies.
- Prepare a meal of their choice. By doing this we are respecting their preference and growing their interest in healthy food.
- Tell some stories and share information relates to healthy food.

- Keep the refrigerator filled with healthy colorful options. The tendency of checking food items kept in the refrigerator will make them natural eaters.
- On weekends invite them to the kitchen and make a meal together. It's a way of spending pleasure time together educating and empowering to make healthy choices in food.

- Maintain a healthy eating schedule and an ideal gap between the meals.
- Offer healthy snacks like cheese cubes, trail mix, oatmeal, whole wheat cakes, whole grain snacks, eggs, guacamole made from avocados, baked potatoes, protein balls, milkshakes, smoothies, etc.
- Prepare a chart of healthy food together. Draw some fruits, veggies, color, or make a thumb impression.
- Teach the table manners and practice together like holding spoons, folk, using napkins, etc.
- We need to be patient with picky eaters. Allow their tummy to feel the craving, the need for food.
- Make a pleasant meal time. Family meals mean talking, relaxing, and spending quality time together.
- Don't make the dining table a battleground. Listen to their tummy and shut out the clean plate rule. Forcing a child to take one more bite, and finish everything will make them erratic eaters and hopelessness towards food.
- Keep them moving to keep them feeding.
- Match colorful fruits and vegetables with rainbow colors. Make them eat each colored food every day. They know the name and they learn the colors.

FOOD PYRAMID
Fats oils a
nd sweets
Milk, Yogurt
and cheese
group
Meat, Poultry,
Fish, Eggs,
Dry beans and
nut group
Vegitable
group
Fruit
group
Bread, Cereal, Rice group
Water

CHAPTER SEVEN

Language Development in early years

Did you hear the crying, cooing, and babbling sounds? These are not just sounds they are the first stages of language development. A zero-to-two-month baby will express its hunger, discomforts, and emotions by simply crying. Smiling back is one of the social gestures that a baby starts from two months. Did your child smile back at you?

Enter Caption

Three to four months baby learns to listen, coordinate with lips and tongue starts babbling. From four to eight months from a single syllable sound, they make multiple syllable sounds. Is your child repeating the syllables you made? like aa, ba, ma, pa, da, ta. So, babbling,smiling and talking with the little ones are the building blocks of language development. The child is looking for a partner to talk to, make silly sounds, to express themselves. Take some time out, come to their world of communication, and imitate and talk to them in their way. Have you seen the hearty smile and the joy of finding someone who's expressing like them?

Many times in public places I came across a Few Months Order's looking at me seeking attention. I ensure I smile back at them and make silly sounds(ba, ma, ca, pa, da) and there you go the million-dollar smile – Makes my day. Parents you also make your day by smiling and babbling with the cutie meatballs.

When we teach our children about good, bad, and right, wrong in our self-righteousness we sometimes shout and use high pitch to drive home the message the child absorbs whenever they want to put across their points. Subconsciously we are what the child is. They can also read you, say you are upset with a sunken face they will snuggle up to you to cheer you up. You might find it annoying but it's their way.

While my stay in America in different places I have observed most American kids are soft-spoken. When I met their parent, I observed they too are soft-spoken. So, this behavior is not out of the world, the child acts like their parents. In our Indian families, most of us scold our children loudly. Many of our children create noise. You know where they are getting from.

Our language is the reflection of ourselves. Language defines who we are, and what we are. For cognitive, social, and literacy development in a child language and communication skills plays a crucial role, especially in the 1st five years of a child's life. From sounds to sentences a child imitates its environment. Watch out parents they are going to absorb every single thing from you without differentiating good or bad. I have friends who have adopted children. The children have mannerisms like their parents. The environment is the KEY.

Some simple suggestions can help you, parents, to make your child a better communicator.

- The journey from blabbering to clear speech demands our attention and involvement.
- Eye contact is a vital tool for boosting confidence while communicating. We always say for interviews to maintain eye contact which shows confidence. This is true for kids too.
- Acknowledge when they call and want to chatter.

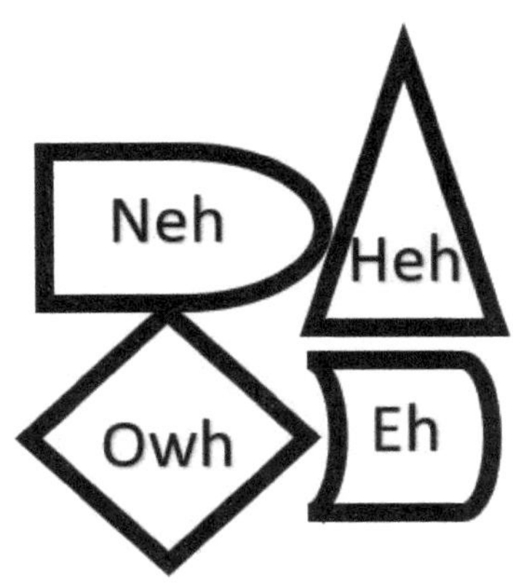

•

- Cheering and Singing songs or rhymes not only makes you and your child joyful but also shoots up their interest in echoing.
- The more you engage your child gets better at expressing his/her basket of emotions.
- Try to answer the silly question of your little ones.
- Listen more, intervene less. Listening encourage them to interact more and express their opinion and viewpoints.
- Keep your words, and sentences clear and simple as they are.

- Gift them every day a bunch of new words.
- Enhance the power of words by repetition.
- Read read and read with them. It can be simple board books, picture books, storybooks, magazine covers, billboards on the roads, or the cover paper of any item.
- Enrich vocabulary by introducing various activities which are realistic.

- First, encourage and then do the correction. It's the learning time so mistakes are obvious.
- Make them social animals. Expand their surroundings beyond the home such as neighbors, social gatherings, and public places, subconsciously those interactions add to their language development. Let them drive their car of thoughts and preferences.

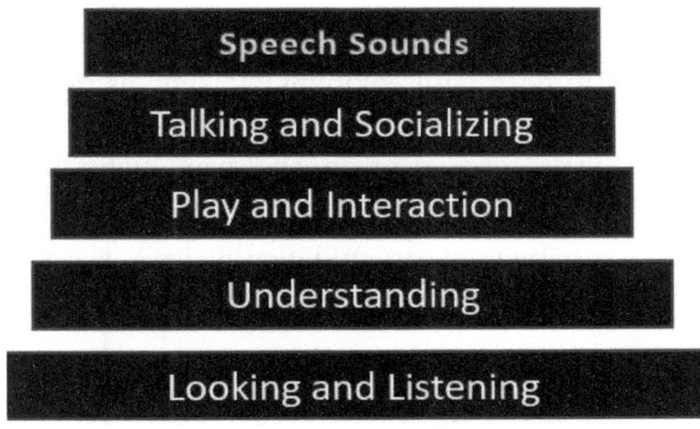

Language Pyramid

CHAPTER EIGHT

Emotion and Socialization

Individuals are born with emotions. As soon as the baby comes out of the mother's womb, he/she starts crying registering their discomfort in the new environment. What's wrong???? Why I am here?? As the temperature outside is less than in the womb, the baby shares its discomfort it's not liking it.

To smoothen the emotion doctors, place the child on the mother's chest so that the familiar heartbeat, the sound, and the warmth helps them calm down. With passing days and months, the baby will evolve with a range of emotions like happiness, sad, anger, fear , envy, and jealousy. Children are like sponges who soak from their environment. Our expression of emotion indicates to the children how to react to a particular situation. When a child gets hurt the parent's reaction to that situation defines how the child will perceive that condition. It is important to self-regulate our emotions in front of the little ones. Parents who stay calm in emergency situations have a sobering effect on the child. Children are able to focus on the task ahead without getting overawed by the gush of emotions. I always suggest parents try not to get panicky or cry or shout when a child gets hurt, it doesn't help the Child. Indeed, we must be calm and relax the child teaching them to deal with situations in a composed way.

Childhood is the right time to bring about emotional maturity as we have more avenues to influence and guide their emotional journey. Thereafter the children outgrow our sphere of influence. Make the hurdles and challenges interesting and adventurous so that they never give up. Encourage positive emotions such as being optimistic, kind, strong, and confident and distract negative emotions anger, fear, and envy which will rule their mind. Children must be put in a position to solve their own problems in their own way and this is possible only when we will make them emotionally balanced i.e., the ability to identify and manage your own emotions and the emotions of others." When they will master this skill, it will make them more socially acceptable.

Emotion is part and parcel of social influence. With self-awareness, they will be more confident, and self-management means the ability to develop a long-lasting meaningful relationships. Emotional regulation is connected with adaptive behavior and easily coping with social demands and challenges. Plant the positive emotions like joy, gratitude, calm, satisfaction, hope, love, forgiveness, interest, and serenity where our little ones will flutter suck, and spread the same to others. Emotional intelligence will make them social butterflies to spread the fragrance of happiness and be happy souls.

Relationship Skills
Decision Making
Self Management
Self Awareness
Social Awareness
Social and Emotional
Learning

CHAPTER NINE

Cognitive Development

In this digital competitive world, our children should be keen observers, good analysts, critical thinkers, and quick problem solvers. We, humans, are not equal but at an early age, it is possible to develop skills and maximize their potential. From the very beginning create an environment that guides them to thrive but remember to make it easy don't push it hard. Children's minds are not cooking pots to be filled but a fire to ignite.

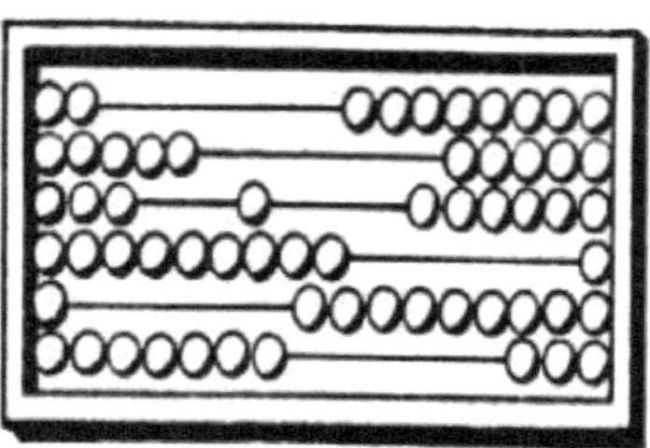

Enter Caption

For cognitive development, the simplest things we need to do are:

Promote self-confidence: Involve children in simple household tasks like mopping, dusting, washing vegetables, non-fire cooking folding clothes, etc... which they crave for. As they see us involved in such activities, they also want to do the same. Though they will make a mess for sure with practice will learn also. Some might say that's really harsh to make these little tiny hands work, just ignore them. It's your child and tomorrow if they are not responsible not sensible and the blame game starts. Engaging them in household chores will definitely make them self-confident, responsible, and better management skills making decisions in the future which are related to cognitive development.

Enter Caption

Engross a child: Anything which is normal is boring for the kids. They always look out for something new and attractive. Can you gift them with new stuff every other day?? Humm.... Not practical. The easiest and the simplest things to do are reading stories, playing hide and seek, making some papercraft,s, etc. which will foster their cognitive skills.

Play with strengths: We all focus on what we like, love, and fascinates us. Success kisses their feet where passion and profession meet. It means talents, and abilities everyone has but not the same. First, recognize we parents and our children are separate individuals. What fascinates us not necessarily will be the same for them. Your choice and his/her choice will most likely differ rarely it will be the same. Secondly, allow them to choose because dumping your choices will be a forceful act that they can't align and the outcome will be zero. Imagine a markup artist playing the role of chef and a cricketer playing chess. Cognitive development means brain development where the likes and dislikes matter because somewhere our mind listens to our heart.

You gift them with more challenges, know their love and passion, develop their knowledge and skills, to know themselves and understand the world around them ignites brain development which is equal to cognitive development.

Why? Where? Who? How?

CHAPTER TEN

Motherhood and Parenting

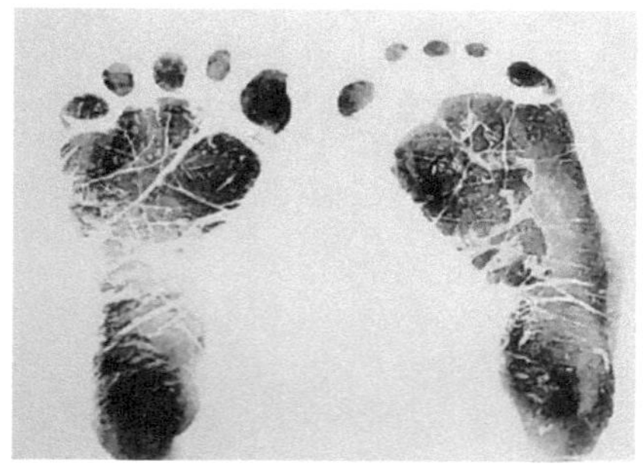

Motherhood is bliss; we women are the chosen ones by nature to carry a life. Becoming a parent is a choice, a choice to be taken when both partners are mentally and emotionally prepared to take the lifelong responsibility. There is no perfect time however unless both have spent enough time to understand the capability between you. Another aspect is to observe physically what you are feeling.

Not everyone has the same journey towards motherhood. In today's time when we are all engrossed in multiple tasks like planning for weekends, attending parties, stay active on socialmedia. Just try to think of a time in the whole week when you are not trying to do anything just lazing around. These moments are far in between since we are so engrossed in tasks, activities, events, and gadgets that an ideal moment seems like a wasted moment. It implies that we subconsciously or otherwise enjoy and invite stress. The stress weall agree is one of our silent partners. It directly or indirectly impacts every aspect of our body composition including our mood, temperament, metabolism,hormones, and overall well-being.

Mothers and Mothers-To-Be is the most important aspect you maylike to focus on. Even the pressure from family members to have a babycan put immenseemotional stress. Counter the pressure and remember, it is your decision to make and not someone else'. A couple must be positive and have a healthy body, mind, and soul, and most importantly stress free. Do not undermine the power of yoga's most inexpensive antidote for a stressful life. This is a gift from our ancestors that the world has adopted wholeheartedly, only we are the hesitant adopters. Something which is simple, easy, and free can also be good.

On the other hand, a career is equally important to all of us. Balancing motherhood and career is a challenge but both can go hand in hand with adjustments.Everybody must play their role to help to bring about that adjustment as a saying goes "It takes a village to raise a child". Mothers you are not alone, everybody likes to be called Grandpa, Grandma, or Papa, let them know their roles to play. They can't match up with your role Mamma because you are the hero of your baby.

"Mother is the first manifestation of power and is considered a higher idea than Father" by Swami Vivekananda.

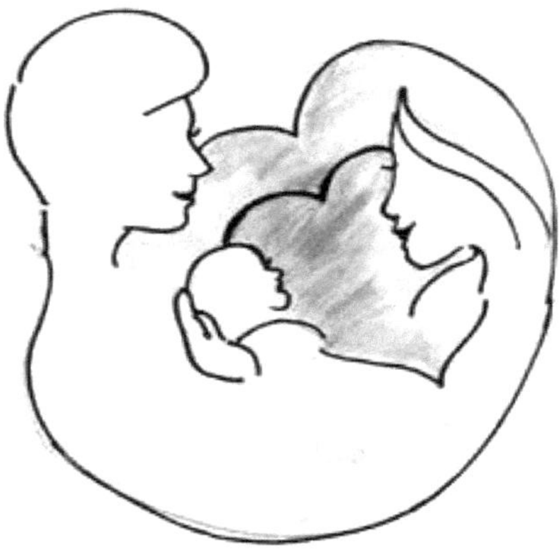

CHAPTER ELEVEN

Quotes On Parenting

"We must help the
Child to act for
himself, will for himself,
Think for himself; this is the art of those who aspire to
serve the spirit"

- Maria Montessori

Children are living beings - more living than grown-up people who have built shells of habit around themselves. Therefore, it is absolutely necessary for their mental health and development that they should not have mere schools for their lessons, but a world whose guiding spirit is personal love

- Rabindranath Tagore

"Knowing that Mother and Father are the visible representatives of God, the householder, always and by all .. Means must please them. If the mother is pleased, and the Father, God is pleased with the man.
That child is really a good child
Who never speaks harsh words to the parents."

- Swami Vivekananda

"There is no school equal to decent home
And no teacher equal to a virtuous parent."
"Every home is a university
And the
Parents are the Teachers"

- Mahatma Gandhi

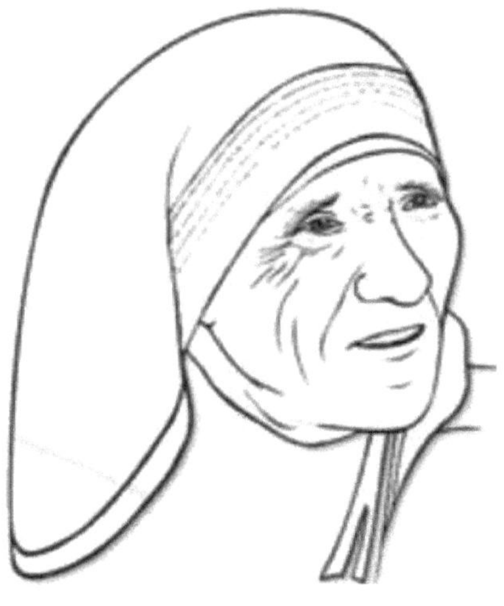

"The Child is the beauty of
God present in the world,
That greatest gift to a family."

- Mother Teresa

"Behind the parents stands the School, and behind the teacher the home

- Abdul Kalam"

Believe In Positive Parenting

Children have little wings
To spread and fly
They are the explorer who always try
If they fall and fail, they will cry
Just guide them right, set them free
To touch the sky

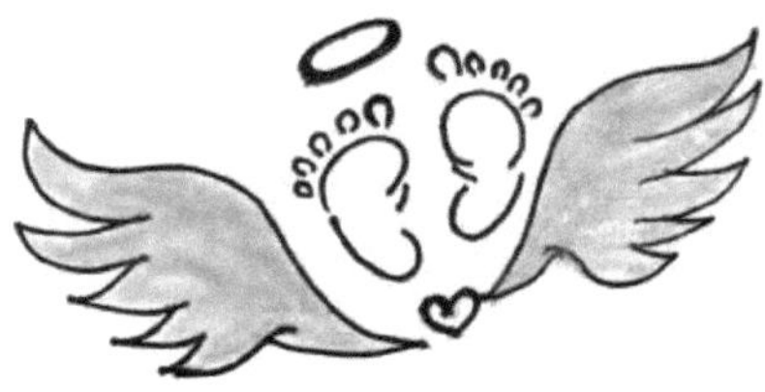

Printed by Libri Plureos GmbH in Hamburg, Germany